POSTCARDS FROM EUREKA

A PHOTOGRAPHIC JOURNEY OF
EUREKA SPRINGS, ARKANSAS

Photographs By Edward C Robison III

FIRST EDITION

© Copyright 2011 by Edward C. Robison III

ISBN: 978-0-615-47929-3

Published by Sacred Earth Press
www.TheSacredEarthGallery.com

Printed in the United States of America

Thank You To The Crescent And Basin Park Hotels For Their Generous Support!

1886 Crescent Hotel And Spa

Built of Arkansas limestone by Irish stonemasons, the 1886 Crescent Hotel & Spa has served as the Crescent College and Conservatory for Young Women for several decades beginning in the early 1900s. In the late 1930s the hotel was purchased by charlatan Norman Baker who duped thousands to the allure of a hope-inspiring yet a never-achieved cancer "cure" when he opened and operated the hotel structure as the Baker's Cancer Curing Hospital.

Today this mountaintop spa resort sits on Eureka Springs' Historic Loop and is surrounded by 15 acres of gardens, forested walking trails, restored Victorian shops, restaurants and galleries. The Crescent hosts more than 300 annual wedding events; and feautures nightly ghost tours prompted by the frequently reported paranormal encounters that rank the hotel as one of the most haunted hotels in the United States. **CRESCENTHOTEL.COM**

1905 Basin Park Hotel

Seven stories of native limestone and pink dolomite, the 1905 Basin Park Hotel, with its jeweled crown of magnificent stained glass windows surrounding the top floor, is the tallest building in historic downtown Eureka Springs. This local landmark, famous for housing the Dalton Gang's Bill Doolin, served the local community as the speakeasy and gathering spot for decades and today proudly continues that tradition. For food, it is now the Balcony Bar & Restaurant. For weddings and galas, it's the Barefoot Ballroom, Atrium and the Ozark Room. For a drink "with a kick", it's where it has always been... the Lucky 7 Rooftop Billards. (even back during prohibition!) Joining locals for everything the Basin Park Hotel now has to offer, like the Serenity Spa and Mountainside Sundeck, are the thousands of visitors who still escape to downtown Eureka looking for fun... served up daily, then and now. **BASINPARK.COM**

INTRODUCTION

In 1998 while I was pursuing a degree in photography at the Kansas City Art Institute a classmate from Fayetteville was telling me about his home state of Arkansas, and the beautiful scenery that filled the state. The following weekend we took a road trip to the Buffalo River, and I immediately fell in love with the incredible landscape I was immersed in. It was then that I knew someday I would live in Arkansas. In 1999 after graduating my wife, Janalee, and I set out to find a place to live in Arkansas. Upon visiting Eureka Springs for the first time we knew right away that Eureka was the artsy town we had been looking for, but timing wasn't right and we needed to find jobs, so we moved to a larger town with more opportunities, Colorado Springs. After a year in Colorado we moved back to Kansas to be closer to family and to start a family of our own, with Eureka always in the back of our minds.

As my photography career in Kansas began to blossom I was offered a full-time photog raphy position at the Nelson-Atkins Museum of Art photographing master works of art. I had already been working as a contract photographer for the museum for several years, and although I really enjoyed the work I could not imagine myself living the fast-paced big city life. So I decided it was time to take a chance on the dream of living in Arkansas and running my own photography gallery. Our family and friends thought we were crazy! In April of 2008 I rented a retail space on Spring Street in the heart of downtown Eureka Springs, and on May 1st I opened my first gallery, The Sacred Earth Gallery (now located on Highway 62 five miles west of town).

Each morning I dropped my son off at school at 8:00am, and the gallery didn't open until 10 am, so I spent my extra morning hours exploring my new surroundings. By bike or on foot, I explored every street and trail I could find. Due to the the heavily wooded and mountainous nature of the town it seemed there was always something new to discover. There are so many secret hidden treasures to be found in Eureka, and even as I write this 3 years later I am still amazed to find new discoveries. Eureka is rich with photographic subject matter, and the only difficult thing about compiling this book was deciding which images to edit out.

So it is my intention, as I write this book, to have it serve as a guidebook if this is your first time in Eureka, or if you are fortunate enough to have made Eureka Springs your home it will remind you of what a special place in which you live.

-Edward C. Robison III
Eureka Springs, Arkansas

BASIN SPRING

Fall at Basin Spring Park

Basin Park is the heart of Eureka Springs. Common ground for locals and visitors alike, and host of musical, artistic and social gatherings.

FLATIRON FLATS

One of the most easily recognizable Eureka Springs landmarks, the Flatiron building stands between Spring and Center streets. It has burned and been rebuilt twice since 1880.

Beaver Lake Sunrise

Early morning colors fill the skies over Beaver Lake 5 miles west of Eureka Springs.

Black Bass Falls

Autumn light dances over the Black Bass Lake spillway. The 200 acre public park offers over 3 miles of hiking trails for visitors to enjoy nature up close.

Rosalie House

Built in 1889, the Rosalie House has been featured in
Architectural Digest and Southern Living magazines.

Basin Park Hotel

Built in 1905, the Basin Park Hotel towers
in the heart of Eureka Springs.

CHARIOTS OF DESIRE

Eureka hosts several downtown parades, but the art car parade
is one that you will surely not want to miss!

The Cat House

With winding roads and scenic beauty at every turn, Eureka Springs draws motorcycle enthusiasts from all over the country. Several motels and eateries display signs advertising, "Bikers Only!"

EMERGENCE

An apparition appears at Cave Springs Cave.

CHRIST OF THE OZARKS

Erected in 1965, the Christ of the Ozarks statue was created by sculptor Emmet Sullivan. The statue weighs 1000 tons and stands 67 feet tall. The height of the original design had to be modified to avoid having to place an aircraft warning light on top.

THE CRESCENT HOTEL FROM EAST MOUNTAIN LOOK OUT

CRESCENT FOUNTAIN

This fountain at the Crescent Hotel serves as a homage to the healing powers of water.

DeVito's

Located on Center Street, DeVito's is synonymous with delicious.

OB-H822

Bavarian Inn

Eureka Springs offers a wide variety of cuisines, including Czech-German at the Bavarian Inn.

A few of the more grim specters of Eureka Springs' past still haunt the streets.

Blocksom & Co. Undertakers and Embalmers

Bank Robbers

Local actors perform a reenactment of a 1923 bank robbery on Spring Street.

WHITE RIVER BEND

Seasons change as the White River bends around Inspiration Point a few miles west of Eureka Springs.

VAN GAIL HOUSE LOVERS

Old World Charm makes
Eureka Springs an enchanting
place for lovers.

HEART FENCE
Home is where the heart is!

CLIFF COTTAGE

Built in the 1880s, Cliff Cottage is a popular Bed and Breakfast Inn.

INN OF THE OZARKS

Inn of the Ozarks is known for its waterwheel,
and the much beloved home-style restaurant, "Myrtie Mae's."

Pathways

Trails, roads and paths wind throughout the town, escaping quickly out of the city and into nature.

"The Flow"

King's River Bluff

HISTORIC HOMES

The entire town of Eureka Springs is on the National Register of Historic Places.

CARRIAGE RIDE

Carriage rides are a relaxing way to pass the time
and enjoy a historic tour of homes.

Sweet's Fudge Kitchen

Storefronts on Spring Street offer sweet nostalgia
alongside the latest trends.

N. A. RAILWAY

OFF

NORTH ARKANSAS RAILWAY

The Eureka Springs and North Arkansas Railway (ES&NA) offers visitors a taste of the past with train rides and exhibits - including an authentic working turntable and a dining car.

QUEEN ANNE MANSION

Gracing the entrance to downtown Eureka Springs is the Queen Anne Mansion. Built in 1891, the mansion was relocated in 1981 from Carthage, Missouri, to Eureka Springs. In its earlier years the Queen Anne hosted such notable guests as Buffalo Bill and Harold Bell Wright. After completing a four-year, multi-million dollar renovation the mansion has recently re-opened for public tours.

Castle Rogue's Manor

Perched on the edge of a cliff overlooking the White River and
the historic town of Beaver, Castle Rogue's Manor is an amazing
home designed and built by Smith Treuer. Smith also owns and operates
the Rogue's Manor Restaurant at Sweet Spring.

Garden Delights

Eureka Springs is full of garden delights. Pictured here are the artistically trimmed hedges at Sweet Spring and living arches spanning the sidewalk between Crescent Spring and the Carnegie Public Library.

BELLADONNA

An extreme wide angle lens was used to capture this unusual view of the Amaryllis Belladonna, also known as the Belladonna Lily, but more commonly known as Naked Ladies. During late July to early August the Naked Ladies make their brief appearance around Eureka Springs. The owner of Belladonna Bed and Breakfast, where this image was created, even hosts a party in their honor. A native to South Africa, the Belladonna seems to enjoy Eureka's mild climate and rocky soils.

Spring & Mountain

Modern mailboxes mingle with the echoes of earlier times at the intersection of Spring and Mountain Streets.

GRAND CENTRAL HOTEL

"The King"

Turpentine Creek Wildlife Refuge provides a haven for "Big Cats"
as well as other animals, and is a popular tourist destination.

GREAT PASSION PLAY

Once making Eureka Springs the most popular tourist destination in Arkansas, the Great Passion Play now lays claim to America's #1 attended outdoor drama.

While visiting the Great Passion Play you can also experience the Museum of Earth History - (Science without Evolution), the Bible Museum, Sacred Arts Center, the Living Bible Tour, Top of the Mountain Dinner Theatre, and see an actual section of the Berlin Wall.

Oil Springs Cascade

Oil Springs is at the beginning of the Black Bass Lake Trail, which will eventually connect with the Master Inter-connect Trail running from Black Bass Lake to the town of Beaver.

MULLADAY HOLLOW BRIDGE

To gain access to the beautiful mountain valley lake at Lake Leatherwood Park
you must first cross the Mulladay Hollow Bridge. The bridge was constructed in
1935 as part of the Civilian Conservation Corps project.

Opera in the Ozarks

Started in 1950 as a summer music camp, the Opera in the Ozarks at
Inspiration Point is now a nationally renowned training facility for opera students.
Open-air theatre productions are performed throughout the summer by aspiring actors.

BLUE BOTTLE SHRINE

In the 18th century, Africans who came to the South as slaves brought with them the tradition of hanging bottles from trees for protection. It was believed bottles sparkling in the sun would lure in evil spirits, trapping them there for all eternity.

Vintage Bicycle

It is estimated that Eureka Springs contains between 50 and 60 miles of locally quarried stone walls. Most of the walls were built between 1885 and 1910.

MORE SHOPS

Eureka Springs is a cross-roads of cultures, and shopping options range from the traditional to the exotic.

DINOSAUR WORLD
Once called "Land of Kong," now defunct Dinosaur World was built by the same artist as the Christ of the Ozarks statue.

PEACEFUL PASSAGE

This vine-covered grotto, one of the many throughout town, is
located near the historic Carnegie Library.

LAKE LEATHERWOOD LOTUS

Lake Leatherwood is a spring-fed lake formed by one of the largest hand-cut limestone dams in the country. The lake is surrounded by over 15 miles of trails that are popular with both hikers and bicyclists.

ST. ELIZABETH'S BELL TOWER
Due to the terrain and setting, the bell tower of St. Elizabeth's
church is also an entrance.

Jesus, "The Keeper"

Dedicated in 1909, St. Elizabeth's Catholic Church was designed after St. Sophia's in Istanbul, Turkey.

REDBUD BLOSSOMS ~ AT BLACK BASS LAKE

Blue Spring Heritage Center

Blue Spring, the second-largest natural spring in Arkansas, and one of the largest on Earth, pumps out over 38 million gallons of water a day. Blue Spring was also a resting place for the Cherokee Indians on the Trail of Tears.

CALIFF SPRING STATUE

Califf Spring, once known as Table Rock Spring, is sheltered
between a rock bluff and what was once the Califf Family home,
Now it is home to the Eureka Springs Historical Museum.

BIRDSONG COTTAGE

Man and nature
peacefully intertwine
at Birdsong Cottage.

CRESCENT HOTEL-1886

Built in 1886, the Crescent Hotel started as a resort hotel. In 1937 "Dr." Norman Baker purchased the "Castle in the Air" and converted it into the Baker Hospital where he treated cancer patients using an elixir of tea brewed from watermelon seed, brown corn silk, alcohol and carbolic acid. In 1940 Baker was sent to Leavenworth Federal Penitentiary for defrauding cancer sufferers out of approximately $4,000,000.

A Christmas Night in Basin Spring Park

REMINISCING.

Tucked away on one of the many steep staircases connecting Spring Street
to Main is Oasis Ark-Mex cuisine, a local favorite.

Palace Bath House

The neon sign at the Palace Hotel and Bath House is said to be the
first installed west of the Mississippi. Completed in 1901, the hotel
was a favorite destination for comedian W.C. Fields.

LITTLE GOLDEN GATE

The Beaver Bridge, built in 1949, spans the White River.
The one-lane, wire suspension bridge is the only one of its kind in
the state of Arkansas still open for vehicular travel.

ANGEL STATUE

"The angels keep their ancient places;
Turn but a stone and start a wing"
-Francis Thompson

GARDEN BRIDGE

Beautiful gardens at the Crescent Hotel provide a place to get away from the fast pace of daily life.

WINTER STRIKES A PEACEFUL CHORD

Autumn in Eureka

Autumn leaves adorn a stone stairway at the Inn of the Ozarks.

THORNCROWN CHAPEL

Designed by renowned architect E. Fay Jones, the Thorncrown
Chapel imparts a sublime tranquility.

SPRING STREET BLUES

Nightlife in Eureka can be fast and colorful.

St. Elizabeth's Church

Italian marble statuettes mark the Stations of the Cross along
the bell tower walkway at St. Elizabeth's Church.

QUIGLEY'S CASTLE

Elise Fiovanti Quigley dreamt of a better house. In 1943 while her husband was at work she tore down their home and moved the entire family of 7 into the chicken house.

When her husband re turned from work he real ized it was time to begin construction on Elise's dream home. The home took 3 years to complete. The exterior is covered in Elise's rock collection and the grounds are graced with numerous paths and gar dens. The "castle" is located 4 miles south of Eureka Springs and is open for public tours.

SPRING GATE

Old and the new exist in harmony.

WINDOW ANGEL

People from all over sing the praises of Eureka Springs.

"Closed"   Downtown Store Window

"DOOR #1"

Secrets are tucked away in every corner & on every street.

Art Horse   Mitchell's Folley

New Delhi Glow

The New Delhi restaurant, a local favorite for Indian cuisine and live music, sparks to life with the glow of Christmas lights, while the Basin Park Hotel towers in the background.

MOONRISE OVER SPRING STREET

Photographer's Notes

Almost all of the photographs in this book were taken with some sort of Canon Digital camera, with the most notable being the incredible Canon 5d Mark II. The background images are a combination of photographs, scans and found textures. Adobe Photoshop was used to layer images with multiple textures to give the appearance of age. Fonts used are Dead Secretary, CheltPress Trial and Aleia.

A Big Thanks!

I want to thank everyone who has helped make this book possible:
My Family - Especially Jana and Ethan Robison
Cory Holbert (who wrote many of the captions)
Rodda Photography (thanks for the many great textures and inspiration)
The Bathkes (For editin' and catching alls my miStakes!)
Steven Ramberg, Mark Feiden, Jodie English, Jeff Cobble....

Fine Art Prints

All of the photographs in the book are available as various sized prints, either with the graphics and aging effects or as traditional straight photographs. For more information or to purchase prints please visit Edward's gallery on Highway 62 West:

Sacred Earth Gallery

15845 Highway 62 West Eureka Springs, Arkansas 72632
www.TheSacredEarthGallery.com
479.253.7644

SACRED EARTH PRESS
www.TheSacredEarthGallery.com